Coping *with* Negativity Yours & Mine *workbook*

Facilitator Reproducible Guided Self-Exploration Activities

Ester R. A. Leutenberg
& John J Liptak, Ed. D.

publisher of therapy, counseling, and self-help resources

Whole Person Associates
101 West 2nd Street, Suite 203
Duluth, MN 55802

800-247-6789

Books@WholePerson com
WholePerson com

Coping with Negativity-Yours & Mine Workbook
Facilitator Reproducible Guided Self-Exploration Activities

Copyright ©2014 by Ester R.A. Leutenberg and John J. Liptak. All rights reserved. Except for short excerpts for review purposes and materials in the assessment, journaling activities, and educational handouts sections, no part of this book may be reproduced or transmitted in any form by any means, electronic or mechanical without permission in writing from the publisher. Self-assessments, exercises, and educational handouts are meant to be photocopied.

All efforts have been made to ensure accuracy of the information contained in this book as of the date published. The author(s) and the publisher expressly disclaim responsibility for any adverse effects arising from the use or application of the information contained herein.-

Printed in the United States of America

Editorial Director: Carlene Sippola
Art Director: Joy Morgan Dey

Library of Congress Control Number: 2013954250
ISBN: 978-1-57025-304-1

Using This Book

Everyone is in a negative or pessimistic mood once in a while. It's a perfectly normal state of mind when it can be overcome. However, when negative moods are excessive, they can be detrimental to reaching full potential and developing and maintaining effective interpersonal relationships. Optimistic people are a pleasure to be with, see the bright side of every situation, and look at the possibilities in any challenge life presents. On the other hand, people who are pessimistic drain others' energy. Negative people complain about everything and are pessimistic about any challenges life presents.

Negative People ...

- Think everything must be perfect.
- Dump on others.
- Feel that things are never good enough.
- Find fault with everything.
- Fail to see the silver lining or possibilities of a situation.
- Display a gloomy outlook on life.
- Say "that will never work."
- Slow other people down who strive to achieve their goals.
- Remain stuck in the past.
- Complain constantly and does nothing to change their situation.
- Shoot down others' ideas.
- Diminishes others' energy level.
- Make others feel badly about themselves.
- Lack insight to see beyond their own problems.
- Expect the worst to happen.
- Live with many negative thoughts.
- Expect the worst so they are not disappointed.
- Have difficulty celebrating their accomplishments or anyone else's.

For many people, the development of a negative mindset coincides with a feeling of life spinning out of control, while for others negativity is a constant in their personality. Researchers have concluded that negativity can be attributed to a personality trait, a negative habit or a combination of both.

A Negative Habit

Some believe that negativity is a habit that people develop over time. In this theory, negativity begins with one negative thought and then snowballs into another negative thought, and so on. Some people become negative as a habit, or an acquired pattern of behavior that eventually becomes involuntary through constant repetition. Therefore, one method of helping people overcome their negativity is to help people break their negativity habit. In essence, people can learn to be more optimistic.

(Continued on the next page)

Using This Book (Continued)

A Personality Trait

Trait-oriented theories of personality description suggest that negativity traits are inherited more often by some people than others. The trait theory suggests that individual personalities are composed of broad dispositions and that a trait can be thought of as a relatively stable characteristic that causes individuals to behave in certain ways. In this theory are cross-cultural enduring traits which can affect the way people think, feel, and behave. In essence, some people inherit more optimistic traits than others.

A Combination of Both Theories:
Negative Habit and Personality Trait

Most current researchers and practitioners believe that a negative life outlook is actually a combination of the two theories. Therefore, all people do inherit certain types of traits that orient them to be more or less negative or positive. As people are exposed to their environments while growing up, they develop habits of being positive or negative. If this is the case, regardless of the negative and positive traits that are inherited, a habit of being negative can be broken and replaced with more positive characteristics.

Negativity

All people are negative at times. However, when negativity becomes part of a person's identity, it can be tiresome for others and difficult to deal with. Trying to stay positive in the presence of someone who is constantly negative can be challenging and can rub off on others.

To deal with their own negativity, it helps people if they engage in the following:

1. Become aware of the extent of their personal negativity.
2. Explore how this negativity affects their relationships, career paths, personal growth and development.
3. Identify methods to overcome negative thoughts, feelings, and behaviors.

In dealing with the negativity of others, it is important to remember that although one may not be able to change the personality of others, one can employ specific tools and techniques to effectively cope with the negativity of others.

The Coping with Negativity – Yours and Mine Workbook helps participants deal more effectively with not only their own negativity, but also with the negativity of others at home, in relationships, in the workplace … anywhere. It provides assessments and self-guided activities to help participants learn useful skills for coping with their own negativity and the negativity of others. A variety of self-exploration activities is provided for participants to determine which best suit their unique needs.

Format of Book

The Coping with Negativity – Yours and Mine Workbook contains assessments and guided self-exploration activities to be used with a variety of populations to help participants cope more effectively with chaos in their lives. Each chapter of this workbook begins with an annotated Table of Contents with notes and examples for the facilitator. Each chapter contains two primary elements: 1) a set of assessments to help participants gather information about themselves in a focused situation, and 2) a set of guided self-exploration activities to help participants process information and learn ways of coping with personal negativity and the negativity of others

Assessments

Each chapter begins with an assessment that provides participants with valuable information about themselves. These assessments help to identify productive and unproductive patterns of behavior and life skills, and to encourage development of an awareness of ways to interact with the world. Assessments provide a path to self-discovery through the participants' exploration of their own unique traits and behaviors. The purpose of these assessments is not to "pigeon-hole" people, but to allow them to explore various elements that are critical for coping with negativity This book contains self-assessments and not tests. Traditional tests measure knowledge or right or wrong responses. For the assessments provided in this book, remind participants that there are no right or wrong answers. These assessments ask only for opinions or attitudes about topics related to a variety of coping skills and abilities.

The assessments in this book are based on self-reported data In other words, the accuracy and usefulness of the information is dependent on the information that participants honestly provide about themselves. All of the assessments in this workbook are designed to be administered, scored, and interpreted by the participants as a starting point for them to begin to learn more about themselves and their coping skills. Remind participants that the assessments are exploratory exercises and not a determination of abilities. Lastly, the assessments are not a substitute for professional assistance. If you feel any of your participants need more assistance than you can provide, please refer them to an appropriate professional.

As your participants begin the assessments in this workbook offer these instructions:
- Take your time. Because there is no time limit for completing the assessments, work at your own pace. Allow yourself time to reflect on your results and how they compare to what you already know about yourself.
- Do not answer the assessments as you think others would like you to answer them or how you think others see you. These assessments are for you to reflect on your life and explore some of the barriers that are keeping you from living a calmer, more rational and less anxious life.
- Assessments are powerful tools if you are honest with yourself. Take your time and be truthful in your responses so that your results are an honest reflection of you. Your level of commitment in completing the assessments honestly will determine how much you learn about yourself.
- Before completing each assessment, be sure to read the instructions. The assessments have similar formats, but they have different scales, responses, scoring instructions and methods for interpretation.
- Finally, remember that learning about yourself should be a positive and motivating experience. Don't stress about taking the assessments or discovering your results. Just respond honestly and learn as much about yourself as you can.

Format of Book (Continued)

Guided Self-Exploration Activities

Guided self-exploration activities are any exercises that assist participants in self-reflection and enhance self-knowledge, identify potential ineffective behaviors, and teach more effective ways of coping. Guided self-exploration is designed to help participants make a series of discoveries that lead to increased social and emotional competencies, as well as to serve as an energizing way to help participants grow personally and professionally. These brief, easy-to-use self-reflection tools are designed to promote insight and self-growth. Many different types of guided self-exploration activities are provided for you to pick and chose the activities most needed by your participants and/or will be most appealing to them. The unique features of self-guided exploration activities make them usable and appropriate for a variety of individual sessions and group sessions.

Features of Guided Self-Exploration Activities

- **Quick, easy and rewarding to use** – These guided self-exploration activities are designed to be an efficient, appealing method for motivating participants to explore information about themselves – including their thoughts, feelings, and behaviors – in a relatively short period of time.

- **Reproducible** – Because the guided self-exploration activities can be reproduced by the facilitator, no more than the one book needs to be purchased. You may photocopy as many items as you wish for your participants. If you want to add or delete words on a page, make one photocopy, white out and/or write your own words, and then make photocopies from your personalized master.

- **Participative** – These guided self-exploration activities help people to focus their attention quickly, aid them in the self-reflection process, and guide them as they learn new and more effective ways of coping.

- **Motivational** – The guided self-exploration activities are designed to be an energizing way for participants to engage in self-reflection and learn about themselves. Various activities are included to enhance the learning process related to developing important social and emotional competency skills.

- **Low risk** – The guided self-exploration activities are designed to be less risky than formal assessments and structured exercises. They are user-friendly, and participants will generally feel rewarded and motivated after completing these activities.

- **Adaptable to a variety of populations** – The guided self-exploration activities can be used with many different populations and can be tailored to meet the needs of the specific population with whom you work.

- **Focused** – Each guided self-exploration activity is designed to focus on a single coping issue, thus enhancing the experience for participants.

- **Flexible** – The guided self-exploration activities are flexible and can be used independently or to supplement other types of interventions.

Chapter Elements

The Coping with Negativity–Yours and Mine Workbook is designed to be used either independently or as part of an integrated curriculum. You may administer any of the assessments and the guided self-exploration activities to an individual or a group with whom you are working, or you may administer any of the activities over one or more days. Feel free to pick and choose those assessments and activities that best fit the outcomes you desire.

The first page of each chapter begins with a Table of Contents annotated with ideas and examples to guide the facilitator.

Assessments – Assessments with scoring directions and interpretation materials begin each chapter. The authors recommend that you begin presenting each topic by asking participants to complete the assessment. Facilitators can choose one or more, or all of the activities relevant to their participants' specific needs and concerns.

Guided Self-Exploration Activities – Practical questions and activities to prompt self-reflection and promote self-understanding are included after each of the assessments. These questions and activities foster introspection and promote pro-social behaviors and coping skills. The activities in this workbook are tied to the assessments so that you can identify and select activities quickly and easily.

The activities are divided into four chapters to help you identify and select assessments easily and quickly:

Chapter 1: Types of Negativity
This chapter helps participants explore how they demonstrate their own negativity.

Chapter 2: Negative Characteristics
This chapter helps participants identify the specific negative characteristics they possess.

Chapter 3: Cope with Your Negativity
This chapter helps participants identify and cope with their own negative attitudes and behaviors.

Chapter 4: Cope with Other's Negativity
This chapter helps participants identify resources for dealing with negativity in other people.

Our thanks to these professionals who make us look good!

Art Director - Joy Dey

Editor and Lifelong Teacher - Eileen Regen

Editorial Director - Carlene Sippola

Proofreader - Jay Leutenberg

Reviewer - Carol Butler

Table of Contents

Types of Negativity Scale

Chapter Table of Contents and Facilitator's Notes 11–12
Types of Negativity Scale Introduction and Directions 13
Types of Negativity Scale 14–15
Scoring Directions. 16
Profile Interpretation 16
Breaking Negative Habits 17
Things I've Never Accomplished .18
Now Get Started! A Make-Over 19
Look for the Silver Lining 20
Acknowledge Myself 21
Sneaky Negative Thoughts 22
Diversions 23
Self-Acceptance 24
My Negative Voice 25
Stop and Smell the Roses 26
Damaged Relationships 27
Time to Reminisce. 28
Selflessness. 29
Have Fun! 30

Negativity Characteristics Scale

Chapter Table of Contents and Facilitator's Notes 31–32
Negativity Characteristics Scale Introduction and Directions 33
Negativity Characteristics Scale 34
Scoring Directions. 35
Profile Interpretation 35
I think I can, I think I can. 36
Separate the Past, Present and Future 37
Positive vs Negative. 38
Get Unstuck. 39
Inspirational Quotations I 40
Inspirational Quotations II 41
Link Positive Thinking with Action 42
See the Bright Side. 43
Label-itis 44
My Imaginary Twin 45
Negativity in Context 46
A Positive Future 47
A Positivity Quotation 48
Achieve Lifelong Goals 49
Compliments 50

Coping with Negativity – Yours & Mine Introduction

Table of Contents (continued)

Cope with Your Negativity

Chapter Table of Contents and Facilitator's Notes 51–52
Cope with Your Negativity Introduction and Directions 53
Cope with Your Negativity Scale. 54–55
Scoring Directions. 56
Profile Interpretation 56
From Failure to Success. 57
Positive Thoughts 58
Self-Fulfilling Prophecy. 59
What Sounds Like Fun? 60
Enjoyable in the Past. 61
A Week of Optimism 62
Mindfulness. 63
Relationship Wrecker 64
Visit an Inspiring Place 65
Negative Inner-Voices 66
Fixate on the Negative. 67
Healthy Positive Focus 68
I'm a Star 69
My Positivity Commercial 70

Coping with Other's Negativity

Chapter Table of Contents and Facilitator's Notes 71–72
Cope with Others' Negativity Introduction and Directions 73
Cope with Others' Negativity Scale. 74
Scoring Directions. 75
Profile Interpretation 75
Positive Qualities of Negative People 76
Negative Remarks 77
Emotional Vampires 78
Avoid Them 79
Be Assertive 80
Replace Negativity with Self-Talk 81
Narratives. 82
A Call to Action 83
Remove Myself Mentally. 84
Exaggerations. 85
Critical Comments 86
Triggers. 87
My Reactions 88
Letter to a Negative Person in My Life 89
A Coping with Negativity – Yours and Mine Quotation 90

Types of Negativity

Table of Contents and Facilitator Notes

Types of Negativity Introduction and Directions 13

Types of Negativity Scale 14–15

Scoring Directions 16

Profile Interpretation 16

Breaking Negative Habits 17

Ask participants to share stories of times when they have tried to break a negative habit. Then discuss the system provided for breaking negative habits.

I've Never Accomplished 18

After participants have completed the handout, ask for volunteers to share examples of things they have not accomplished. Encourage other participants to brainstorm ways that unaccomplished items may be accomplished in the future.

Now Get Started! A Make-Over 19

Ask participants to reflect on what constitutes a make-over. Ask them to brainstorm small changes in their lives that can have a dramatic impact.

Look for the Silver Lining 20

Ask participants for their definition of "a silver lining." After suggestions have been made, share "A silver lining is a hopeful or comforting possibility in the midst of difficulties."

Acknowledge Yourself 21

Ask participants to write about three positive experiences that have happened during their day. Each day, ask participants to share some of what they have written about the evening before.

Sneaky Negative Thought 22

Example:

Where They Occur	What Are These Thoughts	What Are They Related to?
In the kitchen	I'm a terrible cook . . . My food tastes like mud . . .	My spouse psychologically criticizes and abuses me . . . none of these thoughts are accurate!

Diversions 23

After completing the handout, ask for volunteers to tell the group how they divert negative thoughts. Ask the group to develop a list of effective techniques for diverting these thoughts as they occur.

Types of Negativity

Table of Contents and Facilitator Notes

Self-Acceptance 24
Ask participants to look at the various aspects of their lives and identify things about their bodies that they accept, things related to their personalities, behaviors, traits, actions, etc.

My Negative Inner Voice 25
Example:

My Inner Voice Negative Thoughts	To What Situation or Person Does It Apply?	How Can I Replace the Negative Voice With a More Positive Voice?
I'm terrible at school and could never get a college degree.	School	Every time I talk myself out of going back to school, I will say, Stop! You are good at school and can succeed if given an opportunity!

Stop and Smell the Roses 26
After the activity, ask people how they now feel that they are stopping to begin to smell the roses. Ask participants to share their experiences.

Damaged Relationships 27
Example:

Relationship	How I Was Negative	How Negativity Damaged the Relationship
My sister	I always blamed her for not caring enough about dad.	We barely can speak. I want to be less negative with her.

Time To Reminisce 28
Tell participants that reminiscing is "thinking back to positive past experiences that you value." Ask participants to close their eyes and relax, take several deep breaths, and begin to feel calm in their lives. Now ask them to think back over the years to identify stories that define their lives.

Selflessness 29
Example:

Selfless Acts	Whom I Could Help	How I Could Help
Cooking	Sherry, my elderly neighbor	I will begin cooking extra for dinner several nights a week and taking her dinner.

Have Fun! 30
After handouts are completed, it might be interesting to the participants to tally some of the results to identify which of the ways that fun manifests itself most frequently in this group.

Types of Negativity Scale
Introduction and Directions

People who are negative generally fall into four groups based on their attitudes, the ways they think, the manners in which they speak to other people, and ways they behave. The *Types of Negativity Scale* can help you identify your primary negativity type and explore ways of overcoming this negativity.

This assessment contains 28 statements related to the ways you express your negativity. Read each of the statements and decide whether or not the statement describes you. If the statement does describe you, circle the number in the YES column. If the statement does not describe you, circle the number in the NO column.

In the following example, the circled number under YES indicates the statement is descriptive of the person completing the inventory.

	YES	NO
I set goals for myself that I cannot achieve.	(2)	1

This is not a test and there are no right or wrong answers. Do not spend too much time thinking about your answers. Your initial response will be the most true for you.
Be sure to respond to every statement.

Turn to the next page and begin.

Types of Negativity

Types of Negativity Scale

	YES	NO
I set goals for myself that I cannot achieve	2	1
I expect too much from myself	2	1
I expect too much from others	2	1
I rarely think anything is good enough	2	1
I push myself to achieve more and more	2	1
I am never satisfied	2	1
I rarely think I'm good enough	2	1

A - TOTAL _____

	YES	NO
I wait until the last minute to do most everything	2	1
I make the same mistakes over and over again	2	1
I always feel as if I'm in a rut	2	1
I have difficulty in managing my time well	2	1
I never seem to get what I want in life	2	1
I feel like I'm not as good as other people	2	1
I put things off too long and then struggle to get them done	2	1

B - TOTAL _____

Continued on the next page

Types of Negativity Scale *(Continued)*

	YES	NO
I would rather complain than fix something	2	1
I see life as doom and gloom	2	1
I usually expect the worst in most situations	2	1
I often think others' ideas won't work	2	1
I see the glass half empty	2	1
I usually think that situations are hopeless	2	1
I like to minimize others' accomplishments	2	1

P - TOTAL _____

	YES	NO
I am often critical of others	2	1
I often compare myself to others	2	1
I rarely measure up to other people	2	1
I often say "I should have …"	2	1
I am full of regret about my life	2	1
I point out others' mistakes	2	1
I am often my own worst critic	2	1

C - TOTAL _____

Go to the Scoring Directions on the next page

Types of Negativity

Types of Negativity Scale Scoring Directions

The *Types of Negativity Scale* is designed to help you identify the ways that you show your negativity. On the previous two pages, add the numbers that you circled in each section and write the scores on each of the TOTAL lines. You will receive a total in the range from 7 to 14. Then, transfer those numbers to the spaces below.

A - Attitude   Total = _____
B - Behavior   Total = _____
P - Pessimism   Total = _____
C - Criticism   Total = _____

Profile Interpretation

Individual Scale Score	Result	Indications
7 to 9	Low	If you scored in the low range, you do not possess many characteristics of negativity.
10 to 11	Moderate	If you scored in the moderate range, you possess some of the characteristics of negativity.
12 to 14	High	If you scored in the high range, you possess many of the characteristics of negativity.

The exercises in this scale have been designed to encapsulate the different types of negativity identified in the scale. No matter how you scored on the *Types of Negativity Scale* (Low, Moderate or High), you will benefit from doing all of the following exercises.

Types of Negativity Scale Descriptions

A (Attitude) – People scoring high on this scale have a negative attitude. They tend to have high expectations of themselves and others, and believe that people can never live up to these expectations. They are never satisfied in life and always believe that they and others can do more and do it better. They rarely think anything they or others do is good enough.

B (Behavior) – People scoring high on this scale exhibit negative behaviors. They put things off until the last minute, don't feel they are as good as other people, and make many mistakes that they blame on other people. They behave as if they what they want in life is unattainable.

P (Pessimism) – People scoring high on this scale always see the bottle as half empty rather than half full, and tend to see the negative characteristics of any situation. They expect the worst and thrive on defining how even the best plans will not work. They see life as bleak, but would rather complain about it than work to fix it.

C (Criticism) – People scoring high on this scale tend to be very critical. They are critical of other people and themselves. They are their own worst critic and often say things such as "I should have…" or "I wish I had…" They feel like they can never live up to the expectations of others and have regrets about how they have lived their lives.

Breaking Negative Habits

You are capable of breaking your negative habits.
The following system will help you to identify and overcome your negativity.

1) Identify times and or situations when you tend to become negative. What is usually happening at that time?

___

2) Then, identify what is happening to you internally. What are you thinking about?

___

3) Next, identify what begins to happen externally. How do you begin to behave?

___

4) Now, find a replacement for your negative thinking. What could be good replacements for you? What are ways you could begin to be more optimistic?

___

Types of Negativity

I've Never Accomplished

People often become negative when they begin to think about all that they have not accomplished. In the spaces that follow, list those things you never accompl___ and develop a plan for how you might now be able to accomplish them.

I've Never Accomplished	How I Might Accomplish It In The Future

Now Get Started!
A Make-Over

"Our greatness lies not so much in being able to remake the world, as being able to remake ourselves."

– Gandhi

Sometimes you can make simple changes in your life to be less negative.

I would like to give my life a makeover by _____
_____
_____
_____

I would like to do less of _____
_____
_____
_____

I would like to do more of _____
_____
_____
_____

I would like to make the following changes in my relationships _____
_____
_____
_____

I would like to make the following changes in my work or volunteer life _____
_____
_____
_____

Types of Negativity

Look for the Silver Lining

SILVER LINING: a hopeful or comforting possibility in the midst of difficulties.

When you begin to feel negative, it's easy to wallow in your self-pity.
It might help to look for the silver lining of the situation.
Now you try it for your home life.

What Am I Negative About At Home?	My Silver Lining	How Will It Help Me Be More Positive?

Now try it for your work life.
Your work life can include full or part-time jobs,
volunteering experiences, work around your house and/or neighborhood.

What I Become Negative About aA Work	My Silver Lining	How It Will Help Me Be More Positive

Types of Negativity

Acknowledge Yourself

In your journey to become more positive,
you need to learn to notice and affirm the positive experiences in your life.
For the next few days, keep this page beside your bed.
Every evening review your day and write three positive experiences you had that day.

Day	Three Positive Experiences I Had Today
S	1. _____ 2. _____ 3. _____
M	1. _____ 2. _____ 3. _____
T	1. _____ 2. _____ 3. _____
W	1. _____ 2. _____ 3. _____
T	1. _____ 2. _____ 3. _____
F	1. _____ 2. _____ 3. _____
S	1. _____ 2. _____ 3. _____

Types of Negativity

Sneaky Negative Thoughts

If you're not prepared for them, negative thoughts can sneak into your head at the strangest times and places.

What can you learn about yourself from these moments when negative thoughts occur? Complete the following table to identify patterns.

Where Do Negative Thoughts Occur	What Are These Thoughts	What Are They Related To?

What patterns do you notice?

_____
_____
_____
_____

Types of Negativity

Diversions

One of the keys to ridding yourself of your negative thoughts is to divert them to something more positive when they occur.

Check those below that might work for you and write some notes next to them about how to make them work and when.

❏ Say "Go away negative thoughts." _____
_____
_____

❏ Think of happy times in your life. _____
_____
_____

❏ Think of all you have to be grateful for. _____
_____
_____

❏ Replace negative thoughts with more positive ones. _____
_____
_____

❏ Think about people you love. _____
_____
_____

❏ Play with a pet. _____
_____
_____

What are some other ways you can divert your negative thoughts when they occur?
_____
_____
_____
_____

Types of Negativity

Self-Acceptance

Being able to accept yourself as you are is critical in overcoming your negativity.
List the things you accept about yourself,
even if you plan to work on them in the future.

At Home	
At Work	
In Relationships	
Other	

What do you completely satisfied with about yourself? _____
_____
_____

What do you accept about yourself but know you still need to work on? _____
_____
_____

My Negative Inner Voice

We all have negative inner voices that pop into our heads from time to time.
To be more aware of these voices, name them
and be aware of the situations or people they apply to.

My Inner Voice Negative Thoughts	To What Situation or Person Does This Voice Apply?	How Can I Replace These Thoughts With a More Positive Voice?

Notice which situation or person your negative inner-voice focuses on the most. What can you do about that?

_____

_____

Types of Negativity

Stop and Smell the Roses

Positive people are able to stop and smell the roses.
They are able to savor your experiences and stay in the present.
Think about your life and identify some of the experiences
you are having or will have and how you can savor these experiences even more.

Life Role	What I Do	How I Can Savor These Experiences
Family		
Intimate Relationships		
Friendships		
Work or Volunteer		
Leisure Time		
Other		

Types of Negativity

Damaged Relationships

Remind yourself that negativity already has, or soon will,
damage your relationships with others in your life.
Identify the types of relationships you have damaged because of your negativity.

Relationship	How I Was Negative	How This Negativity Damaged the Relationship

Which relationships do you want to work on most to be certain that it doesn't happen again?

_____

_____

_____

Types of Negativity

Time to Reminisce

Whether you reminisce by yourself or with family and friends, thinking back to positive past experiences that you value can remind you of all you have and help you develop a more positive attitude.
Think back over your life and identify the positive experiences you have had.

During This Age	My Positive Experience	How I Can Add This To My Adult Life
Under 5		
6–12		
13–19		
20–29		
30–39		
40–49		
50+		

How does it feel when you reminisce about positive experiences? _____

_____

_____

Selflessness

Plan to do something selfless each week.
Selfless acts are those that you do for other people and expect
absolutely nothing in return.
These acts do not have to be anything major, but ones that are done selflessly.

Selfless Acts	Whom I Could Help	How I Could Help

How can being selfless help you to be a more positive person?

_____
_____

Types of Negativity

Have Fun!

The way we view everyday situations can make for a positive or negative experience.
It can be difficult to stay positive when there is little humor or laughter.
Have fun with these questions and sentence starters.

What fun thing would you like to do that you have never done? _____
_____
_____

Whom can you call to play a board, video or card game? _____
_____
_____

Can you laugh at yourself? Tell a story about it. _____
_____
_____

My favorite comedian is _____
_____
_____

It makes me blush when _____
_____
_____

I'll never forget the day I laughed so hard because _____
_____
_____

As a kid, my favorite comic book was _____
_____
_____

A situation that was embarrassing at the time but is funny now is _____
_____
_____

People who look for humor in a situation tend to have a positive attitude!

Negativity Characteristics

Table of Contents and Facilitator Notes

Negativity Characteristics Introduction and Directions 33

Negativity Characteristics Scale 34

Scoring Directions 35

Profile Interpretation 35

I think I can, I think I can 36
> Remind participants that they are like the little engine that could.
> Ask them to share various stories from different parts of their lives.

Separate the Past, Present, & Future 37
> Share with the group the importance of staying in the present. Explain that the past is gone, and cannot be changed, and the future is far off and may be different than you imagine. Therefore, by only focusing on what is now can people avoid all negative thinking.

Positives and Negatives 38
> Ask if any of the participants are willing to share a personal story about any of their friends, family members, or co-workers who are extremely positive or negative.

Get Unstuck 39
> After participants have completed this activity, ask them to share experiences of getting unstuck.

Inspirational Quotes 40–41
> Share with the group this quote from Bruce Lee: "Cease negative mental chattering. If you think a thing is impossible, you'll make it impossible. Pessimism blunts the tools you need to succeed." Ask participants to describe what the quote means to them.

Link Positive Thinking with Action 42
> Example:

Negative Thought	Positive Thought	Positive Action
I'll never meet anyone to fall in love with.	I'm as lovable as everyone else!	I'm going to the next community social.

See the Bright Side 43
> Example:

I should have . . .	Why I did what I did	How it wound up being okay
Taken that promotion at work.	Wasn't sure I wanted to play the corporate politics.	The person who got the job, now works 70 hours per week. I don't want that.

Negativity Characteristics

Table of Contents and Facilitator Notes

Label-itis 44
Talk to participants about how labeling things as good or bad places an evaluative component on your thinking. Ask participants to share experiences in which they have labeled actions in the past.

My Imaginary Twin 45
Remind participants that when they are writing about their imaginary twin, they are actually writing about their hopes, dreams, and visions.

Negativity in Context 46
Example:

Settings	Ways I Am Positive	Ways I Am Negative
With my partner	I tell him I like his cooking.	I don't tell my partner I appreciate him.

A Positive Future 47
Example:

Roles	Aspects Of My Positive Future	How I Will Achieve It
Home & Family	I want to begin a family.	I will talk with my spouse about how we can financially achieve this.

A Positivity Quotation 48
Ask the group what this quote means to them: "Negativity is an addiction to the bleak shadow that lingers around every human form ... you can transfigure negativity by turning it toward the light of your soul."

Achieve Lifelong Goals 49
Tell group participants that positive people are confident they will be able to work toward and achieve lifelong goals. Thus, optimistic thoughts become self-fulfilling. Ask group members to share their lifelong goals.

Compliments 50
Have group members role play giving and accepting compliments. Ask them to share how it felt.

Negativity Characteristics Scale
Introduction and Directions

Some people have more negative characteristics than others. This scale will assess how negative you tend to be in life. Read each statement carefully. Circle the number of the response that shows how descriptive each statement is of you. Please answer all the questions to the best of your ability using the following scale.

In the following example, the circled 2 indicates that the statement is **Somewhat True** of the person completing the scale.

	True	Somewhat True	Not True
I often find that…			
I expect the worst so I am not disappointed	1	②	3

This is not a test and there are no right or wrong answers. Do not spend too much time thinking about your answers. Your initial response will be the most true for you.
Be sure to respond to every statement.

Turn to the next page and begin.

Negativity Characteristics

Negativity Characteristics Scale

	True	Somewhat True	Not True

I often find that…

	True	Somewhat True	Not True
I expect the worst so I am not disappointed	1	2	3
I am upbeat and happy	3	2	1
I have a gloomy outlook on life	1	2	3
I realize when I am beginning to have negative thoughts	3	2	1
I complain a lot	1	2	3
I look for the silver lining in life	3	2	1
I can easily monitor and correct my negative self-talk	3	2	1
I repeat negative patterns over and over	1	2	3
I look at most things from a positive point of view	3	2	1
When faced with a challenge, my first thought is a negative one	1	2	3
Others say I have a negative attitude	1	2	3
I become upset if I am not perfect	1	2	3
I can control my negative thoughts	3	2	1
When others have ideas, I often say, "it won't work"	1	2	3
I am rarely critical of others	3	2	1
I have trouble celebrating my accomplishments	1	2	3
I put myself down	1	2	3
I like to look on the bright side of life	3	2	1
I feel like I need to be perfect in all I do	1	2	3
I try not to focus on things that didn't go my way	3	2	1
I find fault with little things I do	1	2	3
I think things will never work out for me	1	2	3
I try not to set impossible goals for myself	3	2	1
I find it difficult to laugh, even if others are laughing	1	2	3
I see the possibilities rather than impossibilities	3	2	1

TOTAL = _____

Go to the Scoring Directions on the next page

Negativity Characteristics Scale Scoring Directions

The exploration of just how negative you tend to be is the first step in overcoming negative thoughts, feelings and behaviors. Add the numbers you circled on the scale and write that score on the line marked TOTAL. Then transfer that total to the space below:

My Negative Characteristics Total = _____

Profile Interpretation

Scales Scores	Result	Indications
Scores from 59 to 75	High	If you score in the high range, you seem to not have very many negative characteristics. The exercises will help you maintain your positive attitude.
Scores from 42 to 58	Moderate	If you score in the moderate range, you seem to have some negative characteristics. The exercises that are included will help you be more positive.
Scores from 25 to 41	Low	If you score in the low range, you seem to have many negative characteristics. The good news is that negativity can be overcome.

No matter how you scored, low, moderate or high, you will benefit from these exercises. By going to the next section and completing the activities that follow, you will greatly enhance your chances of coping with your negativity and becoming more positive.

Negativity Characteristics

I think I can, I think I can…

The Little Engine That Could, a beloved children's book, is the ultimate tale of optimism and perseverance. It's an optimistic story that proves that you can be successful by telling yourself, *"I can do it!"*

In the spaces that follow, tell yourself what you can do (that you have not been able to do).

At Home

I think I can… _____
I think I can… _____
I think I can… _____
I think I can… _____

Related to Work

I think I can… _____
I think I can… _____
I think I can… _____
I think I can… _____

In My Relationships

I think I can… _____
I think I can… _____
I think I can… _____
I think I can… _____

In My Personal Life

I think I can… _____
I think I can… _____
I think I can… _____
I think I can… _____

Negativity Characteristics

Separate the Past, Present and Future

Negative people often dwell way too much in the past.
Positive people are able to function in the present and plan for the future.
On the lines below – list what you dwell too much on – in the past, present and future.

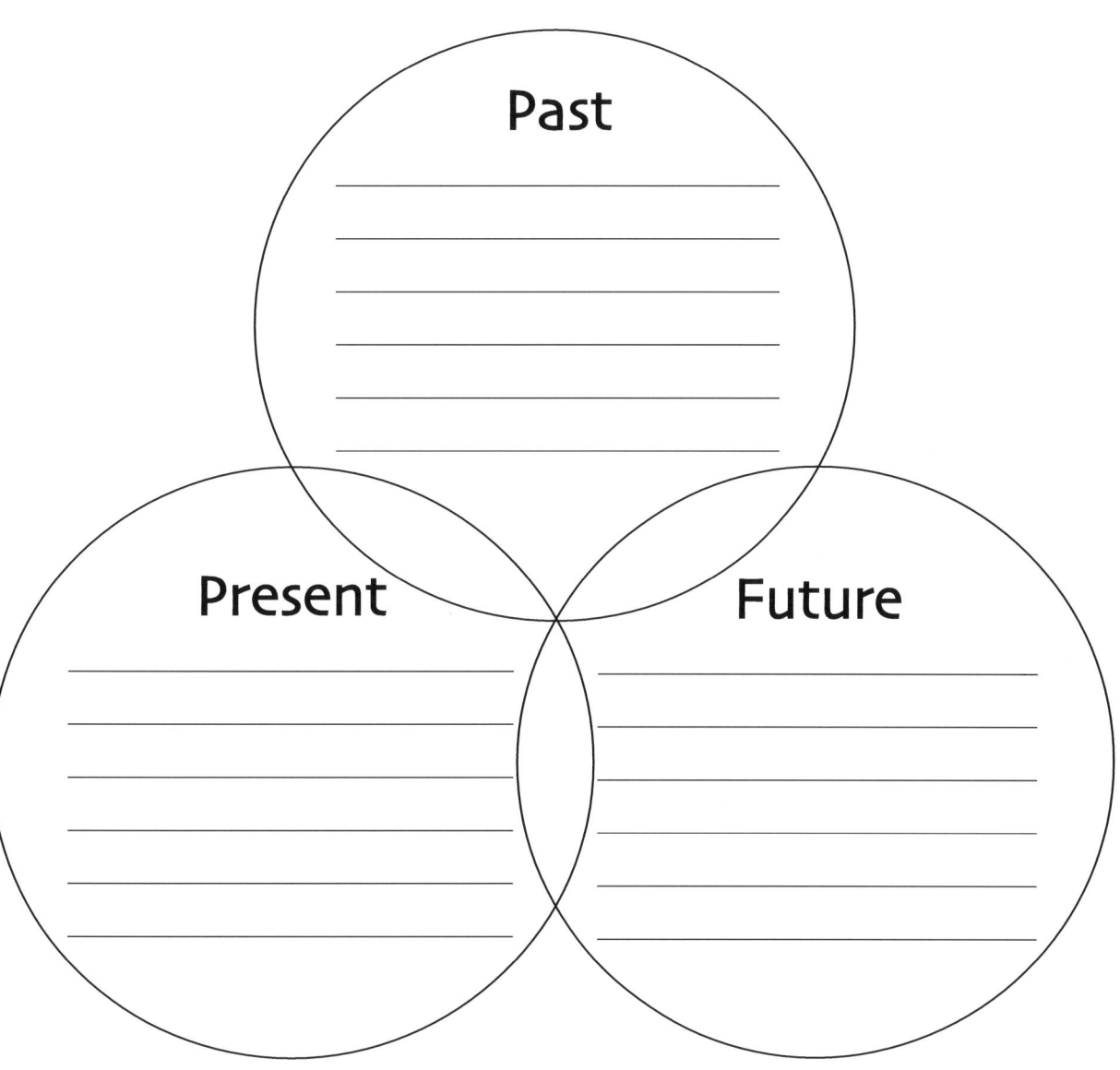

Negativity Characteristics

Positives and Negatives

It is common to have friends, family and co-workers who are positive, upbeat and supportive.
There are probably also people in your life who are negative, gloomy and complain a lot.

In the tables that follow, identify the positive and negative people in your life.

⊕ Positive People

Person	How They Show Their Positivity	How You Feel When You're With Them

⊖ Negative People

Person	How they show their negativity	How you feel when you're with them

Negativity Characteristics

Get Unstuck

When you are stuck in your negative thinking and need to get unstuck, try the following:

1) Identify an important goal that you want to achieve but have been afraid because of because negative doubts and thoughts. _____

2) Identify and list the doubts and thoughts that keep you from attaining your goal.

_____
_____
_____

3) Identify the payoff for attaining your goal:

_____
_____
_____

4) What do you need to do to accomplish your goal?

    a _____
    b _____
    c _____

5) What are the obstacles to accomplishing your goal?

    a _____
    b _____
    c _____

6) What do you need to do to get around the obstacles to accomplish your goal?

    a _____
    b _____
    c _____

Negativity Characteristics

Inspirational Quotations I

Cease negative mental chattering. If you think a thing is impossible, you'll make it impossible. Pessimism blunts the tools you need to succeed.
– Bruce Lee

What does this quotation mean to you?

_____
_____
_____
_____

Write about your mental chattering.

_____
_____
_____
_____

"Once you let go of all the negative people in your life... positive ones appear."
~ Autumn Kohler

What does this quotation mean to you?

_____
_____
_____
_____

Who are the negative people in your life that you can let go of? Why?

_____
_____
_____
_____

(Continued on the next page)

Negativity Characteristics

Inspirational Quotations II

If you accept the expectations of others, especially negative ones, then you never will change the outcome.
— Michael Jordan

What negative expectation of yourself do you accept from others?
_____
_____

Why do accept them?
_____
_____

How can you change the outcome?
_____
_____

I think it's important to get your surroundings as well as yourself into a positive state – meaning surround yourself with positive people, not the kind who are negative and jealous of everything you do.
~ Heidi Klum

Who is negative in your life?
_____
_____

Who is jealous of what you do?
_____
_____

Who are the positive people in your life?
_____
_____

Negativity Characteristics

Link Positive Thinking with Action

It is easy to sabotage positive actions with negative thoughts.
Now is the time to begin to change your negative thoughts to positive thoughts
and then into positive actions. You need a road map for doing so.

Identify some of your positive, uplifting thoughts and tie them to actions you can take.

Negative Thought →	Positive Thought →	✂ Positive Action

Which negative thought do you most want to turn into positive action and how will you do this?

_____

_____

_____

_____

See the Bright Side

Negative thinking often pops into your head
in the form of I should have... However, if you
think it through later, you might realize
why you did what you did, how it wound up being okay,
or how something good actually came out of it.

I Should Have ...	Why I Did What I Did	How It Wound Up Being Okay

Negativity Characteristics

Label-itis

What negative labels do you place on yourself?
List the things you say to yourself when you make a mistake or think you look foolish.

Mistakes I Make	Labels I Put On Myself

ptimistic
My Imaginary Twin

Write a short story about an imaginary twin
whom we will call "the positive you."
Imagine this twin has a positive personality and outlook on life.
In your short story, how does your positive twin act, think, and feel?
Does your twin have different friends and relationships from yours?
Does your twin do different work and activities?
What makes your twin so positive?

When you are writing about your imaginary twin,
you are writing about your hopes and dreams!

Negativity Characteristics

Negativity in Context

Sometimes you may feel optimistic in one setting and negative in another. Identify the ways you are negative and positive in each of the settings listed.

Settings	Ways I Am Positive	Ways I Am Negative
With my partner		
With my children		
With my parents		
With other family members		
With my co-workers or fellow students		
With this group		
With my fellow volunteers		
With my neighbors		
With my community		
With well-meaning strangers		
With others		

A Positive Future

Many negative people are unable to visualize a positive future for themselves. Try to envision a positive future for yourself and the ways you can attain it.

Roles	Aspects of My Positive Future	How I Will Achieve It
Home & Family		
Work & Volunteering		
Friend		
School		
Leisure Activities		
Other		

What do you want to accomplish first to start developing your positive future?

_____

_____

_____

_____

Negativity Characteristics

A Positivity Quotation

> *Negativity is an addiction to the bleak shadow that lingers around every human form . . . you can transfigure negativity by turning it toward the light of your soul.*
>
> – John O'Donohue

What does this quote mean to you? _____
_____
_____
_____

How is negativity an addiction? _____
_____
_____
_____

How does negativity cast a lingering bleak shadow? _____
_____
_____
_____

How can you transfigure negativity in your life? _____
_____
_____
_____

What or who is the light of your soul? _____
_____
_____
_____

Achieve Lifelong Goals

Writing about your goals helps you put together your thoughts
in a coherent manner and thus find meaning in your life experiences.
Positive people are confident they will be able to work toward and achieve lifelong goals.
Thus, optimistic thoughts become self-fulfilling.

What has been one of my lifelong goals?
___
___

Is this goal a possibility?
___
___
___

What are the obstacles to my achieving this goal?
___
___
___

How can I overcome these obstacles?
___
___
___

How can I persist?
___
___
___

Steps I need to take in order to achieve my lifelong goal:
___
___
___
___

Negativity Characteristics

Compliments

Being able to accept compliments will help you develop a more positive attitude. List the types of compliments you receive but have a hard time accepting.

People Who Compliment Me	What They Say	How I Respond To Them and Why

Freely giving compliments will also help you develop a more positive attitude. List the sincere compliments you could give to the people in your life.

People Who Do Something I Admire	What They Do	How I Could Compliment Them

Recognize and Cope with Your Negativity

Table of Contents and Facilitator Notes

Recognize and Cope with Your Negativity
   Introduction and Directions 53
Recognize and Cope with Your Negativity Scale 54–55
Scoring Directions 56
Profile Interpretation 56
From Failure to Success 57

    Example:

Age	How I Was Successful	What I Accomplished
16-30	I sang a solo with my high school choir concert.	I have always been extremely anxious getting up in front of people and I was able to do this!

Positive Thoughts 58

    Example:

Upcoming Challenge	First Negative Thought	Positive Thought
I was asked to speak at a meeting about something I know well.	I get so anxious when speaking in public.	I was able to sing a solo with my high school choir years ago. I can do this now.

Self-Fulfilling Prophecy. 59

   Prior to distributing handouts, explain to the group: A self-fulfilling prophecy is a statement that alters actions and therefore comes true. For example, a person stating "I'm probably going to have a lousy day," might alter this person's actions so that he really will have a lousy day. It may go the other way, also. If a person says "I'm going to have a great day," this person might act in ways that will actually make this come true.

What Sounds Like Fun? 60

   After handouts have been completed, ask for volunteers to share their response the question, "What is your idea of fun?" At the end of the session, ask group if they received good ideas from the others.

Healthy Fun in the Past. 61

   After handouts have been completed, ask for volunteers to share any activities they did in the past that they are now inspired to do now or in the future..

A Week of Optimism. 62

   Distribute this handout, discuss it and ask participants to take it home, fill it in each day and respond to the questions at the bottom. Suggest that this might be something they wish to do as an ongoing activity.

Recognize and Cope with Your Negativity

Table of Contents and Facilitator Notes

Mindfulness 63
Prior to distributing the handout, read Jon Kabat-Zinn's definition of mindfulness to the participants: "Mindfulness means paying attention in a particular way; on purpose, in the present moment, and non-judgmentally."

Relationship Wrecker 64
Example:

Person With Whom I Have a Negative Attitude	Why I Am So Negative With This Person	How It Is Harming Our Relationship
My 85-year old mother	I am her caregiver. She takes a lot of my time. She is demanding at times.	I was always so close with her and our relationship now is tense.

Inspiring, Uplifting, Calming Places 65
Example:

Place Where You Feel Inspired, Uplifted and/or Calm	When and How Often Do You Go There?	What Is So Special About This Place?
A local park	I go once a month or so.	It is beautiful and peaceful. The trees and plants are wonderful. At times children are playing and laughing.

Negative Inner Voices 66
Prior to distributing the handouts, discuss the inner-voice or the internal monologue people here with themselves at a conscious or semi-conscious level.

Fixate on the Negative 67
Example:

What I Feel Is Negative In My Life	How Realistic Is My Thinking	Is There a Positive Side To This?
My relationship with my partner	I dwell on every argument we have and worry that we're over.	I guess it is good that I care and am trying to improve our relationship.

Healthy Positive Focus 68
After the participants have completed the handout, ask for volunteers to share their responses to the last question, "How can you get more positives in your life?"

I'm a Star! 69
Distribute the handouts and explain: "Listing your accomplishments is not bragging or boasting. It is acknowledging and recognizing facets and actions of yourself of which you can be proud."

My Positivity Commercial 70
Prior to distributing handouts, have a discussion with participants of favorite television commercials and why you remember them. Distribute handouts and encourage them to have fun with them. Ask for volunteers who are willing to share their commercials with the group.

Recognize and Cope with Your Negativity Scale Introduction and Directions

All people find themselves being negative from time to time. For some, however, their negativity stops them from enjoying life, developing and maintaining effective relationships, and advancing in a career. The Recognize and Cope with Your Negativity Scale is designed to identify your negativity and learn ways to cope with it.

For each of the items that follow, choose the response that best describes you. In the following example, the circled numbers indicate how much the statement is descriptive of the person completing the inventory.

3 = Very Much Like Me   2 = A Little Like Me   1 = Not At All Like Me

I. When I am at work ...

1. I don't like when anything changes 3   (2)   1
2. I am treated unfairly . . . . (3)   2   1

This is not a test. Since there are no right or wrong answers, do not spend too much time thinking about your answers. Be sure to respond to every statement.

Turn to the next page and begin.

Recognize and Cope with Your Negativity Scale

3 = Very Much Like Me   2 = A Little Like Me   1 = Not At All Like Me

I. When I am at work . . .

1. I don't like when anything changes	3	2	1
2. I am treated unfairly	3	2	1
3. I find fault with my co-workers	3	2	1
4. I always think the work will never get done	3	2	1
5. I expect the worst	3	2	1
6. I find it difficult to see possibilities	3	2	1
7. I complain and give suggestions and no one listens	3	2	1

WORK TOTAL = _____

II. When I am with my loved ones . . .

1. I argue a lot	3	2	1
2. I am gloomy	3	2	1
3. I find fault with most everyone	3	2	1
4. I expect things to go wrong eventually	3	2	1
5. I am usually not interested in their problems	3	2	1
6. I am not supportive	3	2	1
7. I say hurtful things	3	2	1

LOVED ONES TOTAL = _____

Continued on the next page

Recognize and Cope with Your Negativity Scale (Continued)

3 = Very Much Like Me   2 = A Little Like Me   1 = Not At All Like Me

III. When I am with my friends . . .

1. I don't feel good about their successes	3 2 1
2. I often am critical of them	3 2 1
3. I am not very cheerful or pleasant.	3 2 1
4. I say no to others	3 2 1
5. I confront people about things they say	3 2 1
6. I gossip about other friends	3 2 1
7. I often do not agree with my friends	3 2 1

FRIENDS TOTAL = _____

IV. When I am with people in my neighborhood and community . . .

1. I get angry when others don't agree with me	3 2 1
2. I offer to help and support, and then I forget	3 2 1
3. I challenge why people do what they do.	3 2 1
4. I complain a lot.	3 2 1
5. I mind children and pets making noise	3 2 1
6. I have a gloomy attitude.	3 2 1
7. I have many negative thoughts.	3 2 1

PEOPLE IN MY NEIGHBORHOOD AND COMMUNITY TOTAL = _____

Go to the Scoring Directions on the next page

Recognize and Cope with Your Negativity

Recognize and Cope with Your Negativity Scale Scoring Directions

The Recognize and Cope with Your Negativity Scale is designed to measure your negativity in four important aspects of your life: Work, Loved Ones, Friends, and People in My Neighborhood or Community. For each of the sections, count the scores you circled for each of the four sections. Put that total on the line marked "Total" at the end of each section.

Next, transfer your totals to the spaces below. Then add you four scores to identify your Grand Total.

TOTALS

I. _____ = Work

II. _____ = Loved Ones

III. _____ = Friends

IV. _____ = Neighbors and Community Members

_____ = Grand Total

Profile Interpretation

Individual Scales Scores	Grand Total	Result	Indications
Scores from 17 to 21	Scores from 66 to 84	High	If you score in the high range, you have many negative characteristics in the setting.
Scores from 12 to 16	Scores from 47 to 65	Moderate	If you score in the moderate range, you have some negative characteristics in the setting.
Scores from 7 to 11	Scores from 28 to 46	Low	If you score in the low range, you do not have very many negative characteristics in the setting.

No matter how you scored, low, medium or high, you will benefit from the following exercises.

Recognize and Cope with Your Negativity

From Failure to Success

Most people have failed in some way in their past. Failure is nothing to be ashamed of, as long as you don't dwell on your failures, but learn from them and go forward. Thinking about the times when have succeeded throughout your life can help you begin to think more positively.

Age	How I Was Successful	What I Accomplished
0-15		
16-30		
31-45		
46-60		
60-70		
70+		

What do you notice about the connection between your age-range and your successes?

_____

_____

_____

Recognize and Cope with Your Negativity

Positive Thoughts

When faced with a challenge in life, the first thought of many people is a negative one. Think about upcoming challenges you will face, identify your first natural negative thought, and then write a statement that describes how you can replace it with a positive one.

Upcoming Challenge	First Negative Thought	Positive Thought

How do you feel when you replace negative thoughts with positive ones?

_____

_____

Recognize and Cope with Your Negativity

Self-Fulfilling Prophecy

Some people start off their day with a negative attitude. They expect the worst to happen to them. This often becomes a self-fulfilling prophecy. You can begin to live a more optimistic life by starting your day with a variety of positive affirmations. Try the following exercise:

Every morning before you begin your day, stand in front of a mirror in your house and say the following out loud (write your own on the blank lines below):

"I am ready to face the challenges in my life"

"I am a winner"

"I will be positive and optimistic regardless of what happens to me"

"Good things will happen to me"

"I can overcome any obstacles"

"I am expecting the best to happen"

"I will look at the bright side of life"

_____

_____

_____

_____

_____

_____

_____

Recognize and Cope with Your Negativity

What Sounds Like Fun?

By intentionally engaging in activities
that you find enjoyable,
you will begin to think, feel, and act more optimistically.
Answer the following questions to explore your thoughts
about fun in your life.

What did your family do for fun when you were growing up?

_____
_____
_____

What is your idea of fun now?

_____
_____
_____

What obstacles are in the way of you having fun?

_____
_____
_____

Who comes to your mind when you think of someone else having fun? What do they do?

_____
_____
_____

How can you begin to integrate more fun in your life?

_____
_____
_____

Recognize and Cope with Your Negativity

Healthy Fun in the Past

What have you done in the past that was healthy fun – legal, harmless – and fun!

Fun Activity In the Past	Why Was It Fun?	If You're Not Still Doing It, Why Not?

How does having fun help you to have a better attitude?

_____

_____

_____

Recognize and Cope with Your Negativity

A Week of Optimism

Take a week of your life and dedicate it to being optimistic, regardless of what happens to you.

Day	Events That I Would Usually View In a Pessimistic Way	How I Changed My Thinking	How I Felt
Monday			
Tuesday			
Wednesday			
Thursday			
Friday			
Saturday			
Sunday			

How did this experiment work?

_____

_____

_____

What did you learn about optimism?

_____

_____

_____

Recognize and Cope with Your Negativity

Mindfulness

Sometimes life gets so frantic that it is easy to become negative.
Negative expectations will trigger negative emotions and eliminate positive ones.
By staying mindful on the positive, you can let go of negative thoughts
and begin to experience more positive ones.
Try the following:

Become aware of a negative thought as it arises. Write about that thought.

_____
_____
_____

Immediately change the negative thought to a positive one.

_____
_____
_____

Focus on the positive thought!

Notice how the positive thought turns into a positive emotion. Describe what you feel:

_____
_____
_____

Experience it, don't push it away.

Let go of any worries you have. What are the worries you let go?

_____
_____
_____

Stay present with the positive feeling.

Don't let fear get in the way.

Recognize and Cope with Your Negativity

Relationship Wrecker

Consider the effect your negative attitude has on the people around you. You may be pulling them down and holding back the people you love the most by hindering them from living their lives to the fullest.

Person With Whom I Have a Negative Attitude	Why I Am So Negative With This Person	How It Is Harming Our Relationship

How can you begin to repair your most damaged relationship?

_____
_____
_____

Recognize and Cope with Your Negativity

Inspiring, Uplifting, Calming Places

Being in inspiring, uplifting, calming places can help in dealing with your negativity. What are some of these places for you?

Place Where You Feel Inspired, Uplifted and/or Calm	When and How Often Do You Go There?	What Is So Special About This Place?

If you have places – whether they are in your home, neighborhood, outdoors, five minutes from home or further away – and you feel good when you're there, try to go more often!

Recognize and Cope with Your Negativity

Negative Inner Voices

Often times when you hear your negative inner voice, it is not your own thoughts.
It is often the voices of other people who have spoken to you in past times
and these thoughts have stayed with you.
Answer the following questions to identify your negative voices.

My Negative Voices Say…	Whose Voice Is That Connected With?	Write Something That Can Help You Overcome It or Disprove It.

What did you learn about the impact of voices from your past?
_____
_____
_____

Fixate on the Negative

People often fixate on the negative in their lives, rather than focusing on the positive.

What I Feel Is Negative In My Life	How Realistic Is My Thinking?	Is There a Positive Side To This?

What positives came out of this exercise?

_____

_____

_____

Recognize and Cope with Your Negativity

Healthy Positive Focus

People often fixate on the negatives in their lives, rather than focusing on the positives. Identify the positive aspects of your life.

The Positive Aspects Of My Life	Why Do I View This As Positive?	How Does It Feel When I Think About This Aspect?

How can you develop more positives in your life?

_____

_____

_____

Recognize and Cope with Your Negativity

☆☆☆ I'm a Star! ☆☆☆

Make a list of your positive accomplishments. Complete all fifteen!
These accomplishments can be big or small ones.

1. _____
2. _____
3. _____
4. _____
5. _____
6. _____
7. _____
8. _____
9. _____
10. _____
11. _____
12. _____
13. _____
14. _____
15. _____

Put a star by the ones you are most proud of!

My Positivity Commercial

Be creative and write a sixty-second commercial about YOU!
Tell an audience about the positive side of you which might include
your personality, sense of humor, positive communication skills, creative side,
or the way you help or uplift other people.

Cope with Others' Negativity

Table of Contents and Facilitator Notes

Cope with Others' Negativity Introduction and Directions 73
Cope with Others' Negativity Scale 74
Scoring Directions 75
Profile Interpretation 75
Positive Qualities of Negative People 76

A Negative Person In My Life	What Does This Person Do or Say That Is So Negative	Some Of This Person's Good Qualities
My father-in-law	He doesn't spend much time talking with me.	He is amazing with my children; kind, loving and supportive.

Imaginary Remark-Proof Screen 77
After completing the handouts, ask participants to share with the group some of the ways they are able to ignore or deal with remarks that might be hurtful.

Emotional Vampires 78
After completing the handouts, ask participants to share with the group how they can avoid their emotional vampires.

Avoid Them 79
After handouts have been completed, ask for volunteers to share their responses to the last question: "How can you avoid having a lengthy conversation with people you must be together with in a room?"

Be Assertive 80
Prior to distributing the handout, discuss the meaning of 'assertive.' Some aspects are being open, honest and direct; respecting the rights of others and self; speaking clearly and to the point; showing confidence and becoming aware of choices in life.

Replace Negativity with Self-Talk 81
Prior to distributing the handout, discuss the meaning of reframing.
Offer some examples:
"Wow, did I mess up!" – reframed – "I did my best and learned something."
"He made me SO angry!" – reframed – "I chose to let that person get me all upset."
Thomas Edison reframed by saying, "I never failed. I just learned 10,000 things that did not work."

Narratives 82
Divide the willing participants into pairs and ask them to read the completed handout to their partners, and vice versa. Allow them a few minutes to talk about it afterwards.

Cope with Others' Negativity

Table of Contents and Facilitator Notes

A Call to Action...83
Prior to distributing handouts, role-play with a volunteer:
- Trying to FIX someone's problems. (You should tell him you're through!)
- Giving a suggestion and then backing away. (I have a friend who went to a great counselor.)

Remove Yourself Mentally...........................84
Have crayons, markers, pencils, magazines and scissors available (for participants to cut out pictures if they do not wish to draw).

Exaggerations..85
Example:

The Negative Person	Situation This Person is Facing	How This Person Exaggerates
My sister, Jane	Her boss is asking her to take on a new project.	She says "My boss doesn't do anything himself. He gives me ALL of the extra work."

Critical Comments....................................86

Person	How this Person Criticizes You	Reality of the Situation (either positive or negative about you.)
My friend, Bob	He says I never like his ideas.	I don't like many of his ideas but I could be kinder about how I respond to him.

Triggers..87
After handouts are completed, ask for volunteers to role-play one of their situations with another person. (They can go in a corner of the room to prepare.)

My Reactions..88

A Negative Person I Know	How I React	A Better Way to React
Ari, a volunteer at the soup kitchen.	She always asks me to do her job and I tell her, "I have enough to do."	I can say, "If I get all of my work done I can help you."

Letter to a Negative Person in My Life...........89
After distributing handouts, explain to the group that there is great value in writing or journaling your thoughts and getting them off your chest. After they have written their letter, they can send it, put it away for two-weeks and re-read the letter to decide whether to send it or tear it up.

A Negativity (Yours & Mine) Quotation..........90
After handouts are completed, ask for volunteers to share their response to the last question, "How can you make the most of negative situations?"

Read this quotation by Mark Twain, "Keep away from people who try to belittle your ambitions. Small people always do that, but the really great make you feel that you, too, can become great." Ask participants to share examples of this quotation.

Cope with Others' Negativity Scale
Introduction and Directions

The negative people in your life can drain energy and self-confidence from others and discourage and/or influence others' positive attitude. Negative people often blame others for what happens in their own lives, and they complain and see the gloomy side of life. They discourage others from being ambitious, following their dreams and achieving their goals by questioning what they are doing and planting ideas in their head. This scale will help you identify and explore the negative people in your life.

The Cope with Others' Negativity Scale contains 25 statements related to the characteristics of one of the negative people in your life. Choose someone whom you believe, or suspect has a negative influence on you. Answer the questions based on this one person. Photocopy the assessment multiple times if you have more than one person in your life you believe to be negative.

Read each of the statements and decide whether or not the statement describes this person. If the statement does describe this person, circle the number under the YES column next to that item. If the statement does not describe this person, circle the number under the NO column next to that item.

In the following example, the circled number under "Yes" indicates the statement is descriptive of the person completing the self-assessment.

The person in my life who I think is negative: _____

	YES	NO
This person . . .		
Doesn't talk nicely about other people	(1)	2

This is not a test. Since there are no right or wrong answers, do not spend too much time thinking about your answers. Be sure to respond to every statement.

Turn to the next page and begin.

Cope with Others' Negativity

Coping with Others' Negativity Scale

The person in my life who I think is negative: _____

	YES	NO
This person ...		
Doesn't talk nicely about other people	1	2
Puts other people down to feel better	1	2
Attacks the character of other people	1	2
Compliments others	2	1
Criticizes the way things are done	1	2
Sees the gloomy side most situations	1	2
Searches for solutions rather than complaining about a situation	2	1
Has uninterested or defiant body language	1	2
Gossips	1	2
Feels grateful	2	1
Doesn't make excuses	2	1
Rejects new ideas	1	2
Shows no enjoyment of life	1	2
Sees problems as challenges	2	1
Focuses on what's missing in life	1	2
Broods about the past	1	2
Expects the worst to happen	1	2
Contradicts anything said	1	2
Laughs a lot of the time	2	1
Possesses a victim mentality	1	2
Sets and works toward personal goals	2	1
Looks for a quick fix most of the time	1	2
Attracts other complainers	1	2
Sweats the small things	1	2
Sees only what is wrong in people	1	2

TOTAL = _____

Go to the Scoring Directions on the next page

Cope with Others' Negativity Scale Scoring Directions

Negativity in other people can cause you to become more negative. This scale was designed to help you take a look at the other people in your life to determine how negative they are.

For the scale you just completed, add the numbers that you circled. You will get a total in the range from 25 to 50. Put that number in the space marked Total. Then, transfer this total to the space below:

TOTAL = _____

Profile Interpretation

Scale Score	Result	Indications
25 to 33	low	Low scores indicate that this person in your life is negative and will negatively affect your attitude.
34 to 41	moderate	Moderate scores indicate that this person in your life is somewhat negative and might negatively affect your life.
42 to 50	high	High scores indicate that this person in not very negative and will probably not affect your attitude in a negative way.

The following activities are designed to help you learn to better deal with the negative people in your life. Regardless of the scores on the assessment, work through the activities provided.

Cope with Others' Negativity

Positive Qualities of Negative People

List some on the negative people in your life,
how they display their negativity and then, some of their good qualities.

A Negative Person In My Life	What Does This Person Do or Say That Is So Negative?	Some Of This Person's Good Qualities

What did you learn about the negative people around you? Put a check mark by those people whose positive qualities outweigh the negative. Put a star by those who you want to keep in your life no matter what.

_____

_____

_____

Imaginary Remark-Proof Screen

You need to build an imaginary remark-proof screen around you
so that negative comments or remarks from other people cannot penetrate.
Think about the people who give you unwanted negative remarks or comments.

A Person In My Life That Makes Negative Remarks To Me	Typical Remarks This Person Has Made	How I Can Be Sure These Remarks Will Not Bother Me In the Future

Who is a trusted person who might be able to help you if you cannot figure out how to build and use your imaginary remark-proof screen?

_____

_____

Cope with Others' Negativity

Emotional Vampires

Emotional vampires are people in your life who are so negative that they leave you feeling tired, negative, sad or exhausted. In other words, they bring you down rather than lift you up.

My Emotional Vampire	What This Vampire Does	How I Can Cope

How can you avoid these vampires? (Garlic won't work!)

_____

_____

_____

Cope with Others' Negativity

Avoid Them

One way to cope with negative people is to avoid them. There will be some people you cannot avoid (like family members, friends or co-workers), but there are also many that you CAN avoid.
In the table that follows, list the negative people that you can avoid.

Negative People In My Life	How and When I Can Avoid Them	How This Will Help Me

Be creative. How can you avoid having a lengthy conversation with negative people you must be together with in a room? _____

_____

_____

_____

Cope with Others' Negativity

Be Assertive

There may be times when you have heard enough negativity and want to say so.
Think about those times and the other people involved.

The Negative Person	How the Person Showed Negativity in the Past	How I Might Have Been More Assertive

Ways you can be more assertive. Which do you already do?

❑ Speak up assertively without being aggressive.

❑ State your opinion powerfully without being hostile.

❑ Take responsibility and start your statements with "I feel _____."

❑ Express clearly what you want and need.

❑ State your needs in a firm, steady tone.

❑ When saying "No" be decisive and not apologetic.

❑ Resist giving in to interruptions before you state your wants and needs.

❑ Maintain good eye contact and assertive (not passive or aggressive) body language.

❑ Ask for clarification when you need it.

Are you willing to work on any of the above that you did not check? If so, put a check after the sentence.

Cope with Others' Negativity

Replace Negativity with Self-Talk

One way to deal with negative people is to replace their negative statements in your own mind with a positive self-talk response from you.
In the table below, list some of the negative statements you often receive and how you can replace them with positive self-talk responses.

Negative Person's Name and Situation	Negative Person's Negative Statement	My Reframing Response To Myself
Blanche – I showed her my new project	"Oh, it doesn't look like I expected."	That's typical of her. She is always negative. Everyone else encourages my new project.

How can this technique empower you?

_____
_____
_____

Cope with Others' Negativity

Narratives

By sharing a positive experience with a negative person, the story might become an opportunity for personal growth and development for that person. In this method, you can simply listen to the negative person's story, and then share a positive parallel story from your life. Think and write about some of the positive stories from your life that you might like to share with others. Use the back of the page to continue.

Cope with Others' Negativity

A Call to Action

Most negative people would rather complain than try to change the situation.
For them, the focus is primarily on the problem and not the solution.
You may be able to shift a person's focus by suggesting
possible solutions to the problems.
Practice on the items listed below:

Areas of Your Life	This Person's Problems	Possible Suggested Solutions
Person in My Family _____ _____ _____		
My Friends _____ _____ _____		
At Work or Volunteering _____ _____ _____		
In the Community _____ _____ _____		
Other _____ _____ _____		

It is not your job to fix others' problems.
Giving a suggestion might be worth your time. Stay positive and then, back away.

Cope with Others' Negativity

Remove Myself Mentally

If you find yourself in a negative conversation and you cannot remove yourself physically, you might try to remove yourself mentally from the situation. You can let your mind vacate the situation and think about more positive things or places. Draw, doodle or write about the positive things or places you can think about.

Positive Things

Positive Places

Exaggerations

Negative people often exaggerate issues they are facing, thus making their situation seem worse than it is. Look at some negative people in your life, list the situation each is facing and how the person exaggerates it.

The Negative Person	Situation This Person Is Facing	How This Person Exaggerates

What do you realize about the negative people in your life?

_____

_____

_____

Cope with Others' Negativity

Critical Comments

Negative people are often very critical of others. If you have negative people in your life, you have probably had criticisms voiced to you. Identify those people who are most critical of you, how they criticize you, and what the reality of the situation is.

Person	How This Person Criticizes Me	Reality Of the Situation (either positive or negative about me.)

Ways of dealing with critical people in your life:

- Don't take criticism personally.
- Realize the person is voicing an opinion, not facts.
- Identify the underlying message of the criticism.
- Communicate your feelings about the criticism assertively, not passively or aggressively.

Cope with Others' Negativity

Triggers

Negativity in some people is triggered by certain topics.
Switching topics can lighten the mood and lessen the person's negativity.
Think about some of the negative people in your life.
Then try to identify the topics that trigger their negativity.

Person and Situation	Topic That Triggers Negativity	Topic(s) You Can Switch To That Will Interest the Person

Try practicing this technique with someone in the room.

_____

_____

_____

Cope with Others' Negativity

My Reactions

When dealing with negative people, it is important to be aware of how you react to them. By deciding not to react, you can disarm negative people. Think about the negative people you know and describe how you typically react to their negativity. Then identify better ways to react.

A Negative Person I Know	How I React	A Better Way To React

Role-play this technique with someone in the room.

Cope with Others' Negativity

Letter to a Negative Person in My Life

Writing a letter to a negative person in your life can reduce your stress.
This letter can address how the person's negativity affects you.

Dear _____,

When I am around you, I feel your negativity. When you are negative I find myself feeling

_____

_____

_____

_____ .

And I tend to _____

_____

_____

_____ .

I enjoy being around you, but when you become negative you _____

_____

_____ .

I wish that you could be less negative so that we _____

_____

_____

I want to keep you in my life, but your negativity is causing me to become more negative.

_____

SIGNATURE

Cope with Others' Negativity

A Negativity (Yours & Mine) Quotation

> "Negativity sucks away energy. If part of the negativity stems from your attitude or perspective, commit yourself at the beginning of each day and each activity to find something positive in yourself and in others around you. If the people around you are negative and you can't change that, either remove yourself from the situation or view it simply as one obstacle you face in pursuing your own potential. Stay focused on your own goals and make the best of the situation."
>
> – Terry Orlick

What does this quote mean to you? _____
_____
_____
_____

How does negativity suck away your energy? _____
_____
_____
_____

Why is it difficult to change negative people? _____
_____
_____
_____

How do you deal with negative people around you? _____
_____
_____
_____

How can you make the best of a negative situation? _____
_____
_____
_____

Whole Person Associates is the leading publisher of training resources for professionals who empower people to create and maintain healthy lifestyles. Our creative resources will help you work effectively with your clients in the areas of stress management, wellness promotion, mental health and life skills.

Please visit us at our web site: **WholePerson.com**. You can check out our entire line of products, place an order, request our print catalog, and sign up for our monthly special notifications.

Whole Person Associates

800-247-6789